I0799091

A Day to Celebrate

by Jan Stewart
illustrated by Joe Boddy

Practice Decodable 82

McGraw Hill Education

Bothell, WA • Chicago, IL • Columbus, OH • New York, NY

MHEonline.com

Send all inquiries to:
McGraw-Hill Education
8787 Orion Place
Columbus, OH 43240

ISBN: 978-0-02-139021-2
MHID: 0-02-139021-5

Printed in China.

8 9 10 11 12 DSS 27 26 25 24 23

A big picnic takes place every fall at Burns Farm. Farmers celebrate the harvest, rain or shine.

Jay Burns points out the places to park. Little Caleb waves to the cars and trucks as they pass.

Twins Grace and Ava enter the barn with Tad the dog. Mom and Dad stay outside in plain sight.

The barn contains rows and rows of chickens.

Grace and Ava learn that the chickens lay eggs daily.

The sisters walk in stride along the main path.
They did not see the new yellow chick in the hay.

Aiden Burns takes kids for a ride in the cart. Each kid waits for a turn to ride.

The horse trots at a slow pace. Tad races the cart! The cart passes a herd of grazing cattle.

Aiden Burns stops the cart along the trail.
Mason picks an apple from a low branch. Yum!

The farm has tents and stands in the back. Customers may pay for things at the stands.

Stands have jam, potatoes, and hats for sale. Tad stays out of the way behind the man.

Kids eat sandwiches and corn at a picnic table. Tad would like to taste a plate of food!

Kids pet and play with the baby lambs. They are able to feed the little lambs a snack.

The picnic must come to an end. Families pack up for the long way home.

All leave after a good day at Burns Farm. No one has any complaints—only good things to say!